52 Weeks to Fall In Love With Your Money

Apryl Fort-Kelly

ISBN: 1544659067
ISBN 13: 9781544659060

Intro

MONEY WAS MY first childhood boyfriend. It made me feel good. I was happy when money was in my hand because I knew it would treat me well. It would buy me the things that put the biggest smile on my face. Now, don't get me twisted; this was more than a crush--the smile that spread across my lips proved this to be true love. I loved money, and money loved me. From each quarter and each dollar, from soda to shoes, money was "my man" and my man loved me!

I tell you all of this because most of us don't realize the effect our relationship with money has on our lives.

You see, I'd never had money before; so, babysitting my little cousins for five dollars, and cleaning and dusting off my grandmother's baby powder-laced nightstand made this love affair possible. When I was in 7th grade, my Algebra teacher, Mr. Dew, offered fifty cents to whoever could correctly solve difficult math problems. I got them right each time so I could have MONEY! Those two-quarters made me so happy that I equated money with happiness. However, I didn't want the joy all to myself: I would find my older brother, who was in the same math class as I, and offer him the same excitement I got from correctly answering the questions, because I wanted him to also experience the joy of having money for a cold lunchtime Dr. Pepper.

Later, I met a man named Credit Card, and I cheated on Money. I didn't mean to, but Credit Card was so easy. Unlike Money, who often left me working so hard for his affection, Credit Card was as easy as Sunday morning--all I had to do was swipe! After each swipe, I just tucked him away, knowing he was always there when I needed him. All Credit Card requested from me was a small monthly contribution. No pressure--like Money! Money stayed gone when he left, and I had to work so hard to get him back. Credit Card just loved me.

Then, one day I was laid off, and Credit Card turned on me. He wanted his monthly contribution, and I didn't have it. I was unable to give him what he needed, and he became mad! Like a jealous boyfriend, he said, "IF I CAN'T HAVE MY MONTHLY FIX, NO OTHER CREDIT CARD WILL HAVE YOU!" He promised to spread lies that I was no good and report me to anyone who inquired. He was mad and, everywhere I went, other people gave me looks of shame.

Now, I had lost them both: Credit and Money, and I was lost as well. You see, I never meant to do either one of them harm. I loved them both so much and I knew I needed them both, so I came up with something crazy! I explored my financial freaky side and asked Credit and Money to have a threesome. I know, I know, you're thinking: "she is a financial whore." She has been in bed with Money and Credit and, now, she is talking about having them both at the same time!

YES! Yes, I am, and the funny part about this situation is: they agreed! They were happy to assist me in my financially freaky endeavors, and we all fell in love. I learned to keep credit low by paying with money, and I learned to save money for emergencies. Credit and I had a special relationship: he understood that I called him only when I needed him, and that Money was my main dude. Credit was my side dude, but he got to be my hero when I needed him.

All was well--until, one day, I met a stranger who was new and interesting. He sparked my interest when he told me he wanted to take care of me when my money ran out, or when I was old and tired of working. He wanted to be my sugar daddy, and that made me think. He introduced me to his friends and told me that if I hung with him and his crew, I would never worry again. I like not worrying. His friend Roth was so attractive, and 401K was such a good looking brother--he told me I'd never see what I contributed, but that he would show up when I turned 59 ½ to give me back all that I had put in. Brokerage told me he could help me get what they called "dividends," and that it would be extra for me to spend. The gang called themselves Investments, and the dollar sign was their calling card. Getting to know this group made me sleep better and feel more powerful than ever. This group was like no other...

Week 1

Personal Financial Statement: Who Am I, On Paper?

Have you ever seen your reflection in your financial mirror? Consider your Personal Financial Statement (PFS) your financial mirror. Your PFS is a form that tracks your net worth, and it reflects your financial worth. When learning to date your money, you have to know where you stand, just like in any other relationship.

Look in the PFS section of your workbook and follow along to fill out your own PFS.

Question: When you look at your financial reflection, would you date your financial self?

The PFS is one of the most honest statements in the financial world, and it is unforgiving. It will expose you for who you are. Unlike a credit report, which only reports how much you owe and how you pay, the PFS lists assets versus liabilities. The document lists everything: cash, stocks, bonds, and even the cash value of life insurance. The PFS is a complete financial snapshot.

Just like when you're dating, you need some key information.

Question: Can you face the person in the mirror?

Just like realizing you have a lot of work to do when you look in a physical mirror, you have to get in shape financially to have a great relationship with money. Make yourself more attractive to your money. Spruce yourself up financially. Remember, pencils come with erasers because your financial situation is not a permanent one. But, just like getting your body in shape to attract a partner, it will take a financial diet and financial exercise to make you fall in love with the person in the mirror.

Not loving the way you look in the financial mirror? Keep reading! You're going to love your new financial reflection.

Credit Report– The Nosy Friend Who Tells EVERYTHING!

WE ALL HAVE that person in our lives who is always in our business, and who is willing to tell everything they know to anyone who asks. Your credit report is this person in your Credit Dating Life. The problem with these friends is that they sometimes get the information wrong and often paint a picture of you that would surprise even you. They tell the good, the bad, and the ugly--and, the worst part is, they often harp on the past and will bring up old things! Sometimes you have to check these folks!

Week 2- Who Gon Check Me Boo?

You! You have to Check Your Credit Report! Checking your credit report is very important--just like checking that friend in your life. It's never good to have anyone spreading lies about you. Clearing up false information on your report will help your overall credit health. Also, just like in your personal dating world, you have to get rid of your past. You should report anything over seven years old as dated to the credit reporting company so that these items can then be removed from your report.

You never need deadbeats hanging around, trying to tell a story of the old you. These deadbeats, of course, were lessons learned--you have grown from your past, and you are ready to face new financial challenges. Cleaning up your report is very important.

Your credit report says a lot about you, so keep it clean and nice. It's often your first impression to the credit world. Think of it like going on a date with someone with a dirty car: they come to pick you up, and all are you are thinking about is if your outfit will get dirty in their car. When this happens, you are unlikely to want to date them again. The cleaner the credit report, the easier it is for a creditor to cut to the chase and see a good review of your credit history. Never underestimate the power of being simple and clean--it means a lot in the credit world.

Week 3- Taking Out the Trash

We know we have to clean up the report--but what, exactly, does this mean? Well, it means you need to take out the trash on your report. You always want a clean house; you never know when you make want to invite someone over for a night cap. Same with credit; you always want to keep a clean report, because you never know when you may need to run your credit. So let's start with some housekeeping rules.

Rule #1: Nothing should be over the limit! Over-the-limit accounts hurt you a lot. These accounts drastically affect your credit score. I call this the dishes of credit. A kitchen should stay clean because a dirty kitchen is an eyesore that makes you think a person is nasty. Same way with your credit dating world: over-the-limit accounts make you appear irresponsible, and are eyesores to potential creditors.

Rule #2: No More Late Payments! Nobody likes a person who arrives late for anything! Just like you wouldn't want to wait for your date, creditors do not like to wait for their payments. Late payments make you seem irresponsible, and can make a creditor think that timely bill payments are not your priority, which is a red flag for someone whose objective is for you to pay them back! So, ashes to ashes... dust to Late Payments!

Rule 3: No balances over 30%. That's right. Yep, I said it. Let me say it again. There will be no balances over 30%. If we must carry a balance on our credit cards, we need to get them down as low as possible--definitely lower than 30%. Did you know that high balance credit cards pull your score down tremendously? Credit is like sports: the more points, the better. So, to win this credit game, you must shoot for the stars. If you cannot pay the balance in full, pay as much of it as possible and try not to charge over 30% on any of your charge accounts. If you are able to pay a chunk of your balances down below the 30%, you will see a leap in your score, which will also help your Debt to Income (DTI). Put that in your pocket for later--we will come back to that. Yes, we are going to get *REAL* in the next 52 Weeks.

Week 4: Where'd You Come From?

We all have those numbers inside our phones that we have to give the side-eye. The side-eye is the confused look you give when you are not sure where, when, or why something is happening, or where something came from. You're really not sure who this person is, or why their number is in your phone, or if you've ever even spoken to them. Usually, this is someone you meet at the club: they said, "let me give you my number," and you meant to delete later, but forgot. Or, it's someone you thought was cute but, when you actually spoke to them, you realized they were in the friend category. They weren't bad people; you just found something more interesting to do.

In the credit world, these are called dormant accounts. Nine times out of ten, you haven't used any of these accounts since college, or they are accounts you opened to get discounts or free t-shirts from stores you never shop at anymore, or which have gone out of business. These accounts usually have a zero balance and are just hanging out on your credit report. These accounts eat up your DTI and take up a lot of space on your credit report. These accounts can be easily closed with calls to customer service. If it has been a period of time and the creditor has closed it for you, you just need to ask for an account closure letter, which you will then submit to the credit bureau for the account to be removed from your credit. This is a simple task and will take you no time.

Nobody likes a credit troll. These accounts are the freeloaders of the credit report. They make you look like you have too much credit in the credit world and like you have cards everywhere. This reminds you of the guy or girl that has too many friends of the opposite sex. She or he may not have jumped in the bed with any of them, but just because they are hanging out, people assume they have or will. This is a major turn-off for your potential future mate and now you have missed out on a great relationship. Same with credit: you can have too much. Too many credit cards can be scary to a lender. Even though you have a zero balance, the lender assumes you could be tempted to use the cards.

<u>Week 5: Why You Bringing Up Old Stuff?</u>

Let's face the music, we all have pasts, and some of them stink! Ok, now that we've gotten that out the way, we have to do something with these old accounts, just like we have to let go of baggage from past mates! I know they cheated, hurt your feelings, called you fat, said, "I needed bigger 'this' or smaller 'that'... I know--we all have heard it and, trust me, all of these things hurt; and, they are jerks for saying or doing whatever it is they have said or done. I totally agree, but it's time to move on! Same with collection accounts. You have to look at each one differently to determine your course of action. Just like people: you may leave some and never look back; some, may motivate you to get in the gym and get super fine; or, some, you may choose to live with.

<u>The New New</u>, They are the ones are hurting you now. Call the company to see if you can make an arrangement. Ask if, upon full payment, they would remove the account from your credit report. If they say no, you have the option to pay it--but, note: it will still report as a collection, just a paid one that won't bring down your score. Sometimes, this will work but note: this is a hit or miss, and you can call the company to try to pay them directly. When you do this, you can contact tell the collection company you have paid them in full, and you are demanding its removal from your report. They will ask for proof or even check with the company first, but they will remove it. These are the ones you want to get rid of quickly. You're a grown up now, and you don't need anyone ruining your credit name.

<u>The Old Heads</u>, These accounts have been on your credit for years. I do mean years! Bothering them is like waking a grumpy bear. If you make payment arrangements with this grumpy bear, they will start to report again and ruin your credit. If these accounts are seven years old or older, you can write to the credit bureau and ask for them to be removed. Most credit bureau sites have dispute forms through which you can request the removal of accounts over seven years old. These accounts remind you of that person you went out with a long time ago, who still wants to tell everyone who has ears that you went on a date with them! The sad part is: you have moved on, cleaned yourself up, removed that tongue ring, started a new life, and forgotten all about them! Just being seen speaking to this person may spark many conversations about you, so you politely wave and keep it moving--and, you only even do that *if* they make eye contact. If

not, just let them sail into the sunset. These accounts are not bringing down your score anymore, and that person is not blowing up your phone anymore! Once every seven years, make sure you get them deleted just like you did the memory of your horrible date!

Then, you have <u>The Stalkers</u>! The stalkers will send mail requesting for you to make deals with you on twenty-year-old accounts--or, they call, saying you owe them from something you can't even remember. In the dating world, these are the people who send you friend requests on social media that make you wonder where they got your information and why are they requesting you now, after all these years. You barely remember them, but they are quick to tell you how you dated when in reality: you went out to eat with them in college because they were paying! No judgment; we've all had the pity meal with that one person--or, if you were smart, you said, "I would love to go out with you but, I have a test tomorrow, and I have to study. I'm super hungry, but I really need to study because I've been slacking, can you drop me something by?" When they got there, you gave them a five-minute conversation at the door, then you were back to relaxing--I mean, studying! You simply don't reply to these type of accounts, and you rarely see them on the credit reports, unless you make arrangements with them. Just stay away and, if they do decide to report, make sure you send the credit bureau a letter if it has been seven years since your last account activity.

Week 7: Is That A Read?

Like attempting to understand the opposite sex, reading and understanding your Credit Report isn't always an easy task. There are symbols and codes that will give hints about your financial habits. The credit report will spill the tea, aka tell your business, each time.

For instance, the credit report bureau list will list every one of your financial accounts that are reported to the credit companies. Experian, Equifax, and Transunion are the nosiest people in your neighborhood--they are worse than the little old lady peeking out of the window! They know all your business and don't mind telling it! So, you really have to watch who you bring into your financial world--and, you'd better treat them right because they are going to REPORT IT!

Here's how to understand the signs, or the shade, a credit report is throwing at you: if you are late, the credit report is sure to tell everyone. Next, to each line item, you will find a number. These numbers will show you how many days you were late. If you have never been late it may just have a 1, to show a payment was made. Now, if you were 30 days late, it will have a 2 to represent how many days you were late; a 3 to represent 60 days late; and, so forth. Some credit reports are a little bit shadier and will put you on Front Street and list 30, 60, 90 to represent the number of days late. This type of report says it and says it loud: "You were [this] late, for [this] long, and it was not cute!" In the dating world, this reminds you of the two types of people who post on social media after a date. One person will post "Guess time is not important to everyone," and will say it without saying it; but, you always have the other type of person, who says, "I can't believe So-and-So is 75 minutes late. It's 8:15pm and they were supposed to have been here at 7 o'clock."

The moral of this story is: if you want to fall in love with your money, be on time. It will save you a lot of money, and your money will love you back. In the dating world, you have to make up by buying gifts, etc, when you're late--well, in the financial dating world, you will pay with the gift of late fees. Some late fees range from $25 dollars and above!

So, I know some of you are fashionably late, which works for some accounts. For instance, a car, a house, and some installment debts--put that in your back pocket, we will take it out later--will allow you a grace period. These periods vary, but 10 days is usually the standard grace period. Revolving debt--put that in your other pocket--is just the opposite. This debt has to be paid on, or before, the due date and often has a cut-off time. Have you ever received a late fee because you paid your credit card bill after 5pm on the due date? We all have! Revolving due dates have no mercy, so it is always better to pay before. This is no different from the dating world: we all have dated that person who is timely and will have an attitude all night because you were late; and, we've dated that person who is more laid back and totally understanding of your late habits--unless you're super late, in which case, you are definitely in trouble. Both of these people exist in the financial world as well. The best advice I can give you is: know who you are dealing with in both worlds!

<u>Week 8: HOW DO I FIX THIS</u>

We just took a look at the past mates on our roster. We know who is not good for us and who we need to get rid of. We even discovered the relationships that were worth holding on to and developing. Our last step in finding our financial dream date is to fix the things wrong with our financial reputation. You know: clean it up and make ourselves look good to the financial world. This won't be easy, and it will take months before anyone believes that we have changed, but it is worth it--trust and believe me. Let's recap what we need to do to clean up our credit profile:

- Pay all charge or credit card accounts to under 30%
- Remove all dormant accounts
- Contact Equifax, Experian, and Transunion about collections over seven years old
- Get rid of collection accounts
- No more late payments! Or late fees!

These helpful tips will help to clean yourself up and make you more attractive to potential creditors. There is nothing sexier than a person who keeps their credit clean.

Speaking of clean credit, did you know that an inquiry can make you seem like a bad person to financially date in the credit world? Yes, creditors are funny about you asking too many people for money. Worst of all they even dock you points for that. It reminds you of the person who wants to be in a relationship with everyone. They seem a little desperate. We all have that friend that has had a crush on EVERYONE! No one wants to be in a serious relationship with this person because they have been with all of the friends in the circle. In the credit world, too many sweethearts can lead to deducted points and creditors not wanting to be in a financial relationship with you. So, choose who you have run your credit wisely because nobody wants to be in a credit relationship with someone who tries to hop in the credit bedroom with everyone!

Week 9: What's Your Number?

These days, people are more interested in your credit score than your phone number. Back in the day, people would ask, "What's your sign?" Now, people want to know, "What's your score?" No matter your astrology sign, a low credit score is a stop sign for a financial lover.

"What is a low score?" You may ask. That is a great question. Credit scores, sometimes called FICO Scores, range from 600 to 850. Anything below 600 is bad; you have made lots of mistakes in the eyes of the credit world; 600-649 is considered Poor. You have done some things wrong, but you have a little good in you; 650-699 is considered Fair. You're not a horrible person to date financially, but you know to keep your eyes open; 700-749 you have Good Credit. You are like the princess of credit. You do right by your credit and you are worth dating financially. If you have a score of 750- 850 you are credit Royalty! You're like a credit superstar and the paparazzi are looking for you. You probably get a lot of credit card offers in the mail and people want you!

Now there are many types of credit scores. Potential credit partners have the opportunity to use scoring models such as FICO, Vantage, Vantage Score scales 1.0, 2.0 and 3.0, Plus Score, TransRisk Score, Equifax Credit Score. The same rules apply to all of these models: the higher the score the lower the risk. Just like in dating, you're more likely to want to date a 10 than someone you would consider a 1.

Week 10: So How Do I Come Up?

Just like in your dating world, you do things to make yourself more attractive to your potential mate. If you wear glasses, you may remove them to give yourself a fresh look. Well, this same rule applies to the credit dating world. You have already cleaned yourself up--now, you have to spruce yourself up. So, this week, we are getting a credit makeover to make our scores look sexier than ever!

Monday: We are going to check our Debt to Income Ratio (DTI) to make sure we don't have too much credit. Like in the dating world, we don't want to be so clingy as to rely on credit for everything. A good DTI is 30% but, the lower, the better! No one likes a person who always has too much baggage. Too much debt is always too much drama!

Tuesday: Remember, you will still need to use your cards. Yes, you heard it right; you still need a payment history, so you still need your cards! Charge your card for small things, and pay it in full monthly. Bring the card to a zero balance each month, and you will see a big difference in your score in 6 months. Like flirting in the dating world, everyone still needs to know they got it--just don't go overboard, as you can easily turn off both a potential credit mate and a financial mate!

Wednesday: If you don't have a card, GET ONE! You will need revolving credit to raise your score. Most banks offer a secured product that will allow you to put a few hundred down to receive a card that will allow you to start your new credit relationship.

Thursday: Now, this one is a little credit secret that will help you upgrade your credit life quickly. This tip is like the push-up bra of credit. Add yourself as an authorized user of card belonging to someone with great credit, who you can trust to continue to make their payments. Note: If you add yourself, you must know and trust this person completely and know they have never been late! Once you add yourself to this card, you are going to get their entire credit history! Proceed with this step carefully. It reminds you of going on a blind date: you will walk into the situation based on what someone has told you about their account.

Friday: Check your credit limits. Make sure your limits match. Lower limits are easier to reach, and you don't want creditors feeling that you swipe to the limit each month. Just like in the dating world, you don't want your future financial soul mate to think you're a heavy spender when you really have a higher limit. This, also, is reflected in your score.

Saturday: Raise your limit. Just like those new jeans, you want your credit to fit, but not too tightly. Raising your limits will help your score, especially if you were close to the limit. You just went from using 50% of your limit to 30% in a matter of minutes! Be careful not to charge more on this card with your newfound limit.

Whew, that was a week filled with a lot of homework. We are trying to get ourselves prepared for our potential financial love connection. Finding true love always starts from within, just like in the dating world. We are learning to love our financial selves and it feels good! Rest, my dear, it's been a week! See you next week!

Week 11- DATE NIGHT!

NOW THAT YOUR credit is all cleaned up and spruced up, it's time to work on your flaws. For instance, we need to work trimming our financial fat! We have to work on our budget. The credit report was like cleaning up your past dating record, and the budget will help you in your future. The word "budget" makes some people shake with fear but, the reality is, a budget can be your best friend. Just like when you're working out to get your body ready for dating, you may have a trainer or an accountability partner; your budget is your financial accountability partner. Your budget is that one friend who will let you know a guy is a loser!

There are a few key items that you should look for when finding your budget:

- **Needs:** What are the things in your life you need, such as mortgage, car, insurance, food, etc.?
  Remember, people: designer shoes and clothes are not needs. Save those for the "wants" chapter.
- **Savings:** We can all save, and saving is different for everyone. No matter if it is $5 or $1,000, as long as you are putting it to the side. I always suggest opening an account that is dedicated to savings. This account should not have a debit card or ATM card. No easy access!
- **Miscellaneous:** This is for those little things you may have to have to be happy. For instance, I love soda and chocolate. I budget for these every month, under miscellaneous. Also, I have kids; so, I make sure I keep cash budgeted in my purse so I can be a mom but stay on track.

Look, your budget is not to make you too miserable to enjoy your life. As your accountability partner, it is there to tell you if you are spending too much money. Think of your budget as your sober friend of the financial dating world. When you have had one too many, your budget will let you know you have reached your limit, and it is time to bring it on home. No potential financial date wants a person who doesn't know their limits!

Think about your budget the way it is now. Write down the following:

Mortgage/Rent: _____ (include insurance)

Utilities: _____ (include water, gas, etc.)

Car/Transportation: _____ (include car payment, insurance, and gas)

Food: _____ (include groceries and takeout)

Savings: _____ (do not include 401K's and any pre-taxed accounts)

Personal Debt: _____(include credit cards and monthly loan payments)

Entertainment: _____ (include the fun stuff)

Other: _____ (include donations, clothing, etc.)

Week 12- Know When To Say When

Just like when you're on a date, you have to have your limits. No matter if you're drinking or eating cake, you have to know your limits when dealing with your budget. You will need to set saving goals. Don't get me wrong: you should never stop saving. Things will happen--it's called life--and you will need your savings to help you through these moments. Always continue to build, because you never know when life will happen. But, this week, we need to decide how much you need to be you and put together a savings goal strategy. This reminds you of writing down what you want in a mate and what it will take for you to be the perfect mate. In this case, we are writing down our expenses and putting them into categories to determine how much can be spent in each category.

Mortgage/Rent, including insurance, is 25%

Utilities, including water and gas, etc. should be 8%

Car/Transportation, including car payments, insurance, and gas, should be 15%

Food, including groceries and takeout, should be 15%

Savings, not including 401K's and any pre-taxed accounts, should be 10%

Personal Debt, including credit cards and monthly loan payments, should be 12%

Entertainment, the fun stuff, should be 5%

Other, including donations, clothing, memberships, should be no more than 10%

Now that you know your limits, take the time to trim the fat off your budget to fit. Just like your favorite pair of jeans, you may have to squeeze into your budget, but you will eventually work off the additional fat to fit into your budget comfortably.

Week 13- Rainy Day and Emergency Fund

We all have that person we call when we are between relationships. I call them your Stan, meaning your standby conversations for those late nights when you need someone to talk to. If you, like most of us, have more than one of these people, you can call.

The one you call that you chat with that is nothing more than a chat: I mean, you have absolutely no intention to actually go out with this person or even see them--this is your Rainy Day Fund. This account is there when your car breaks down, needs tires, or you have a small and unexpected expense. These accounts should be funded with $1000 and are for small, unexpected expenses. Remember, tickets to see your favorite artist or new shoes are not considered emergencies!

Put these funds in an interest-bearing savings account--and, if you ever take the funds out, make a plan to replace the funds immediately. An easy way to save these funds is to deposit $100 per paycheck into your savings account and watch it grow! You will have your account funded in no time!

Emergency Funds are for your big emergencies, such as a job loss or a medical emergency. This account should fund with 6 months of expenses. It will take longer to fund this account. These funds can be placed in a brokerage account to earn interest. Please be sure to let your advisor know you are looking for funds you could retrieve if needed. You don't want to pay penalties if you ever need your money--this would be like being asked on a date and paying for it, too. You ask and you pay; I deposit and you pay! It's only fair!

Some quick tips to save for both your rainy day and emergency funds:

1. Take your lunch: twice a week, brown bag it and put the money you usually would spend on lunch into a savings account. This doesn't seem like a lot but, in a year, you will have your rainy day fund complete.

2. Have $50 automatically placed into a separate account. This account should have no ATM card and should not be easily accessible. This account should be a money market so you gain interest as you go. Remember, your interest won't seem like much at all in the beginning. It may be a few pennies if that. But the golden rule to money is, "Pennies Make Dollars" this is true dating world in a sense that "The Small Things are What Count." If you can have the mindset that all money is good money, no matter how large or small, you will soon see your financial love affair change.

3. Swear jars and Keep the Change jars work as well. At my house, we do Dimes for Disney: all of our dimes go into a jar that will help the kids get to Disney. If you have children, and you are able to commit to filling two two-liter bottles with dimes, you could raise approximately $700! This works for your rainy day fund, emergency fund, or vacation fund. This is a fun and easy way to save as a family!

4. Your Network can increase your net worth, so try earning extra funds from your hobby. Selling Avon, Mary Kay, vacations, and other network marketing can be easy ways to earn for a rainy day and for emergencies.

Now, it's time for action! Write three ideas that you can utilize to help you save: I will fund my Emergency Fund by: (6 months of expenses)

1. _____
    _____

2. _____
    _____

3. _____
    _____

I will fund my rainy day fund by: ($1,000.00)

1. _____
   _____
2. _____
   _____
3. _____
   _____

I'm your financial dating accountability partner. Remember, just like in the dating world, you need that friend to help keep you in check and let you know when you've found the right one or when you've found the wrong one!

Week 14- Speed Dating

Have you ever been speed dating? During Speed Dating, you go from seat to seat and table to table, meeting guys or girls for no more than two minutes to see if you would like to learn more about them. This week, we are going to go on financial speed dates to quickly eliminate your debt. I know nobody wants to spend their lives with debt--which is why, this week, we are going to visit our past to see who we can get rid of, and who gets to hang around a little longer. The Revolvers are the first dates we will meet at the table, and we need to get them in and out as soon as possible. These accounts usually carry baggage, such as higher interest rates and high late fees. Then, we work on our Installers: these accounts, such as your home, will stick around for a while.

The Game Plan is simple: we are going to start by getting rid of the lowest amounts owed. These are the dates to whom your greetings are fleeting, because you know you're not interested in further pursuing them.

Review your credit report, catalog your debt by amount, and plan to attack the lowest. Remember, long-term installment accounts, like your home and car, should be set aside for now.

Financial Speed Dating Round 1: You have placed the accounts in order-- now, let's plan our dates.

- Date One should be the lowest amount with the lowest interest rate
- Date Two should be anything under $100. Plan to pay those off with your next check. You don't want to risk late fees, or continue to earn interest on these accounts. Interest on such a low amount of money is giving away money. Nobody wants to date a person who gives it up that easily!
- Then, we proceed in order, paying off one account at a time. Paying off debt is like being free to date as many people as you like; there is nothing wrong with paying off more than one debt at a time. You're not in a committed financial relationship, and your future financial soul mate will be happy you have gotten rid of this financial baggage.

Quick Tip: I like to create debt-boards that help me envision myself debt-free. Take a piece of cardboard and write out all the companies you owe. Have fun with this step: you can place them on a drawing of a track, as if this is a race to the finish line, or any other creative way you would like to express getting rid of your debt. Personally, I like to use the dating technique! Draw a picture of each of your potential dates on an aisle. Each potential date should represent a debt that you owe. I like to have two separate boards: one for revolvers, and one for installers. At the end of the aisle, have a ring in the box or a heart. You can now work your way to the ring. Each debt you pay, you can now cross off your list. Once all your debts are paid, you are ready to be financially engaged.

Week 13- Bank Accounts and Money Market VS Savings Accounts and Checking Accounts

The first rule of finance is YOU NEVER LEAVE MORE MONEY THAN NEEDED IN YOUR CHECKING ACCOUNT! Most checking accounts earn little interest, if any, so having money stay in these accounts is useless. A Money Market account will gain interest that will help you produce those dividends that you deserve. Savings accounts were, at one time, lacking in interest compared to Money Market accounts--but, as of lately, you will find that more savings accounts are carrying higher interest rates.

Just like in your dating life, play the field. Do a search on the different financial institutions and discover which account is suitable for you. There is nothing wrong with going a financial date to see which institution works best for you but, be sure to read the bottom line when you're ready for your financial hookup! Some accounts require a minimum deposit, may have a monthly fee, or even have penalties if you have too many transactions. Yeah, some accounts are like finding out the person you thought was your soul mate is really a crazy person!

This week, do your research! Just like when meeting a new person, it's always good to Google them first and check with friends and family to see if they know anything about them. In other words, go to streets and get opinions on the service of the bank, as well as going to the bank and forming your own opinion. Google can be your best friend in your financial love life!

Here we go again; I am your nosy homegirl, ready to help through your dating life.

Write down 3 financial institutions at which you would like to open a savings or money market account. Also, check your current institution and compare with two others.

1. Name:_____
    Money Market Interest Rate:_____
    Fee: _____
    Average Daily Balance Required:_____
2. Name:_____
    Money Market Interest Rate:_____
    Fee: _____
    Average Daily Balance Required: _____
3. Name:_____
    Money Market Interest Rate:_____
    Fee: _____
    Average Daily Balance Required:_____

Take this week to compare the accounts, review the perks of each one, and decide if you would like to open an account in which to place your Emergency Fund and/or Rainy Day fund. It's always good to have these accounts at separate institutions, so you are not tempted to take the money when you are handling your everyday transactions.

Week 14- Sacrifice For Love

This week might be a tough one. I am asking you to go into your personal space, look deep into your closet for anything you are not wearing--bags you do not carry, baby clothes the kids have outgrown, and jewelry you no longer wear--and pull it all out, because you are looking at gold!

This will be a way for you to find your financial love. You can take these things to consignment stores or, if you're web-savvy, list them for sale on sites like Tradesy, Amazon, Ebay, and or Craigslist. It's a simple and easy way to pay off debt.

List the items you are willing to do away with:

1. _____
2. _____
3. _____
4. _____
5. _____
6. _____
7. _____
8. _____
9. _____
10. _____

Life Insurance (Covered) The Ultimate Help Mate

Week 15- How much do I need?

LIFE INSURANCE IS a tricky and, sometimes, scary topic--it's like asking someone if they want kids. If your biological clock is ticking and you are ready for children, you are not interested in just dating forever. You are ready to get a ring, a house, a baby, and a minivan. Just like with kids, most people try to get life insurance when it's too late! It usually happens when, one day, they look up and realize that they may need to leave something for their families. The sad part is: once you're sick, or of certain age, life insurance policies become more expensive.

Everyone should have a private life insurance policy. Employer-provided life insurance is great if you plan on working for your employer until you die--most people want to retire. If you retire, you have to reapply for life insurance, independently of your employer, and your rates will go through the roof!

So Rule #1: ALWAYS GET AN OUTSIDE POLICY! Think of it as having your own place and your own money while you date someone--the worst thing is when someone thinks they've met their soul mate, but are left broke and hungry after a messy breakup with an ex they were depending on.

Time for some action! This week, call five Life Insurance companies. These companies can be referrals from friends and family; results from a google search; or, simply, a television or radio commercial. List your five insurance "blind dates" here. You just need their names and numbers; we have to get ready for our date before we call them, so hold tight.

	Name	Phone Number
1.	_____	_____
2.	_____	_____
3.	_____	_____
4.	_____	_____
5.	_____	_____

Week 16- Term vs Whole Life Insurance

There are different types of life insurance, just like there are different types of soul mates, and each serves a different purpose.

There are a few different Insurance mates to consider:

Whole Life, aka Cash Value Life Insurance (CVLI), is like a marriage: it will be with you until death do you part. Like most life insurance policies, CVLI pays out upon death. The key to this policy is value accumulation--that's right, this policy gives the gift of cash! The interest and earnings on this policy are not taxable, which makes it a worthy potential soul mate. As the policyholder, you can choose the cash sheltered investment, which you can use to pay the premium, borrow from, or pass to your kids to create generational wealth. What a mate! A policy that is in this relationship for life, gives you a stash for later in life, and will be there for your kids? I think I just got googly eyes!

Term Life Insurance is the player of the bunch. This type of life insurance will live with you for 30 years, but will not marry you. It is considered the straight shooter of life insurance and will only payout if death occurs during the term, just like a date who will only pay if they asked you out to eat.

Level Term and Decreasing Term are the twins of Life Insurance. Level Term is the consistent one who will pay out the same benefit and be attentive to all your needs for the entire time you are together. Decreasing Term is the twin who slacks off year over year. For as long as you're together, the death benefit drops in yearly increments.

Time to work: choose which policy works best for you and your family!

I think I would like _____ type of insurance. I will ask my agent about this insurance.

As a parent or spouse, we do not want the church to have to have a fish fry to bury us and take care of our family. Do more research on each policy and carefully choose which one works best for you. We all know we will die one day--just make sure you leave your family in a great situation.

Week 17- How to Choose An Agent

It's no secret that insurance agents are everywhere. There are billboard signs, TV commercials, radio commercials--and, some of us still get the door hangers! A knowledgeable and trustworthy insurance agent is very important. The agent is your financial matchmaker. They will introduce you to different products and help you find a love connection.

This week, you will identify 5 agents to interview. Earlier, you wrote down the companies; now, it is time to find the right *representative* best suited to you.

Name	Phone Number
1. _____	_____
2. _____	_____
3. _____	_____
4. _____	_____
5. _____	_____

Insurance is there to help if something happens to you or your car, home, rental, etc, and your agent is there to tell you if you have too much or too little insurance. This person is your plug into the insurance world, so you need to trust them.

Week 18- How Much?

What if you were to die today? It's an uncomfortable thought to entertain, but it is necessary. This week, we will calculate how much would it take for your family to survive without you.

First, consider your final expenses. If you want an extravagant homegoing ceremony, then you will need more life insurance--but, if you'd prefer a simpler ceremony, you will need less. This is a totally personal decision but, remember:

you really won't be there to enjoy it so, maybe, rethink that gold-plated casket and the horse-drawn carriage.

Final Expenses $_____ (Write an estimated amount for your final expenses)

Second, catalog any outstanding debts.

Outstanding Debts $_____(Write the total current debt, not including your mortgage)

Third, evaluate your mortgage and your current payoff.

Mortgage $_____ (If your account is not escrowed, be sure to include your taxes for the next 5 years)

The sum of the listed is what your family would need to survive, in the event of your death. If you have children, I recommend also factoring the cost of four years of college tuition. This can be tricky since costs could rise, but a start is better than nothing at all.

Credit Cards- Your Ultimate Side Piece
Week 19- Living Life with credit cards

Credit Cards are the ultimate side piece for many reasons. You will always love cash. Cash is your best friend. Most of us want to keep it close, and we hate to see it go. However, we all know cash is a rolling stone that always has a place to go. Cash can only take care of things *when it is around*. For many people, cash is hard to keep. We even try to hide our cash behind a debit card, under the mistaken assumption that if we can't see it, we won't spend it as quickly. However, most of us swipe without even knowing our available balance.

Swiping too much can get you in a lot of trouble, especially if it's a credit card--it's like taking a person on so many dates that they assume they're in a relationship with you when, in reality, you just enjoy their platonic friendship. Once you swipe your credit card too many times without the cash to back it up, you're stuck together. You are now committed--in some cases, until death do you part!

It's easy to minimize a credit card's potential impact: you pay a small monthly contribution, and you get all the things you want now. It even seems thoughtful when a credit card company offers interest-free rates for ninety days or longer. This is great--*if* you can pay it back in ninety days. If not, your credit card can quickly turn into the houseguest who overstays their welcome; you invited them over for the weekend and, three months later, they still have their toothbrush in your bathroom.

This week, your action plan is to evaluate your active credit cards: write down their names, the amount owed, and the interest rate. The goal is to differentiate your long-term loves from the charge-it-and-quit-it cards.

Card Name	Number	Balance	Interest Rate

Week 20- I Don't Need You

Unfortunately, we all need a credit card. I know some of us are very independent and think we can be alone forever, but you will crave attention from someone else eventually. We all need people, and we all need credit. Credit cards can help keep a high credit score high, but the key is to maintain a low balance. The best way to keep a credit card in check is to keep your balance below 30% and pay it off to a zero balance.

You need revolving credit to complete your financial love affair so, if you don't currently have revolving credit, you should establish a way to obtain a credit account.

This week's action plan is to obtain a credit card account. Here are a few ways to do so:

- Apply for a credit account at your local bank. Local credit unions and banks both have credit cards for which you can apply, so speak to a customer service agent.
- Apply online with companies such as Capital One, American Express, Discover, and/or CitiBank--alternately, visit a site like cards.com to find the card that best fits your needs.

- Secured cards are for those who may have blemishes on their credit histories. These cards are "secured" with a deposit that becomes your credit limit--so, when you put down a $500 deposit, your credit limit becomes $500, and you are issued a card.
- Become an authorized user of someone else's credit account. If your mate has a good credit history and has never made a late payment, hop onto their credit account to gain their credit history.

Remember, benefits are dependent on your credit type and vary from card to card. A good credit score might qualify you for zero-interest payments, cash back, and/or airline miles. Please note that some accounts may have annual fees and other hidden costs. This week, make sure you do your research; you want to make sure the card you pick has perks. It's like meeting a new mate and discovering he or she is a millionaire! Sure, you were just looking for someone who was faithful, trustworthy, and funny--but, there's nothing wrong with a little added bonus.

List 5 credit card accounts that are potential soul mates. Remember, terms and conditions will always vary--even for secured accounts--so, you want to make sure you research interest rates and hidden fees.

	Credit Company	Interest Rate	Annual Fee (Yes or No)
1.	_____	_____	_____
2.	_____	_____	_____
3.	_____	_____	_____
4.	_____	_____	_____
5.	_____	_____	_____

Week 21- Identify Yourself

There are two types of people in the credit world: the Revolvers and the Closers. The Revolvers always carry a balance, while the Closers pay each account to a zero balance each month. It's fine to be a Revolver--just be aware that you need to keep your account balances under 30%. This may mean restricting yourself to only charging up to 30% on each account--instead of overspending and then stressing to pay the balance down to 30%. This doesn't mean that you should get multiple accounts, to which you only charge 30% each--I know you thought about it! Remember, having too many credit accounts (especially too many new ones) can hurt your score.

When you're dating, you don't look for multiple people to be your one perfect mate. Can you imagine how much that would cost you? Dinners, dates, gifts, and quality time--alone--would be a fortune. It's the same in the financial world: too many credit cards with different interest rates, penalty fees, and miscellaneous hidden fees can quickly become overwhelming.

This week is a little different in our book. This might be an "off" week for you, or it might be a buckle-down week. List all of your revolving debt balances and evaluate how close you are to 30%. If you are above 30%, you need to make a big effort to pay these accounts down below the 30% mark.

Credit Account	Limit	30%	Current Balance

If you have more credit accounts than the space allows, please continue on a separate sheet. We want to make sure we are tackling *all* credit accounts.

Week 22- Give me a little Sugar

As you mature in your financial life and start to look for a long-time soul mate, you might want to consider investment accounts--I call them the sugar daddies or sugar mommas of the financial world. I know that after saving, paying off debt, and bringing all credit accounts below 30%, investment accounts might seem a little counterintuitive, but--don't worry, investing and saving can go hand-in-hand.

There are fifteen types of retirement plans: IRAs, Roth IRAs, 401(k) Plans, 403(b) Plans, Simple IRA Plans, SEP Plans, SARSEP Plans, Payroll Deduction

IRAs, Profit-Sharing Plans, Defined Benefit Plans, Money Purchase Plans, Employee Stock Ownership Plans, Governmental Plans, 457 Plans, and 409A Nonqualified Deferred Compensation Plans. Don't they sound sexy? These are the mates that will take care of you when you are old and grey.

The first sugar daddy is the 401(k), which allows you to contribute a portion of your wages to an individual plan while you are an employee. Most employers offer a 401(k) to full time employees--take full advantage when offered. The key is to max out your plan's potential. Your employer may also offer a match, which you should take advantage of, because it's free money! You don't have to be someone else's employee to have a 401(k) plan--small business owners can also take advantage.

This plan is good if you are a bad saver; the deductions are pre-taxed and automatically withdrawn if you are an employee. Also, a 401(k) will allow you to borrow against the funds within your account, in the case of a lull in cash flow or an emergency. I recommend that you never do this! When you borrow against a 401(k), you borrow your own money--but, you pay interest to the plan's administrator. Also, withdrawing the funds before the age of 59.5 subjects you to a 10% penalty.

Week 23- Brokerage Accounts

A Brokerage account is the super hot superstar of the financial world. It looks and sounds good. When you hear wealthy people talk on TV, you hear them speak about their brokers and their brokerage accounts and how they invested and made millions. It's like they're dating Beyonce; great looks, great body, great voice, and great wealth!

By definition, a brokerage account is a taxable account you open with a stockbroker at a brokerage firm. The account is funded with cash, a check, or an automatic withdrawal from a checking or savings account. Once the account is funded, you can buy stocks, bonds, etc, and your broker earns a commission whenever you buy or sell.

There are two types of brokers: traditional and discount. A traditional broker offers full service; they are the date who opens doors, pulls out your chair, *and* pays for dinner. A discount broker only executes trading and will NOT give advice; they are the person you meet at the bar for good conversation, but you pick up the tab. Either broker is fine; the choice simply depends on where you are in *your* financial dating life.

It's important to find a broker you can trust, which is why, this week, we are going to speed date brokers. List five brokers you're interested in. Tell them exactly how much you have to invest, and ask about strategies to maximize your funds.

1. _____
2. _____
3. _____
4. _____
5. _____

Week 24- You and Money Can Be Happy Together

They say money can't buy you happiness--however, reducing your financial stress by getting your money together can definitely make you happy. Financial polls have indicated that 7 out of 10 people stress over money; and, 1 of 10 say they stress over finances, period. Stress can lead to lack of sleep and depression, and can drive people to unhealthy coping mechanisms like overeating, drinking, smoking, etc.

Here are some examples of ways to help reduce your stress over money:

1. Live within your means. Stress can make you overspend, and there is nothing worse than wondering how, or when, you can pay a bill.
2. Reduce debt by being energy efficient: set your thermostat to 77 degrees and turn off extraneous lights and appliances.
3. Make a shopping list to save on gas from return trips, and take advantage of coupons for extra savings.
4. Save on eating out by brown-bagging your lunches. If you meal prep, this can also help you shed some pounds.
5. Cut cable costs by investing in other forms of television such as an Amazon Firestick or Netflix--we all know how great Netflix and chill nights can be.

Now, list some of your own examples of ways to reduce debt and financial stress that will work for your life:

1. _____
2. _____
3. _____
4. _____
5. _____

Week 25- Whaddya Mean

Credit is a foreign language and, this week, I am your financial translator so, here are financial formulas that will help you navigate the credit application process.

Cash Flow = Income - Expenses

Understanding your cash flow means knowing what it truly takes to be your best financial self. A negative cash flow lets you know to pay off debt and/or identify supplementary income sources.

Leverage Ratio = Debt / Income

"Leverage" is to use borrowed money. Your leverage ratio is how much debt you're in. A lot of people are over leveraged. A good leverage ratio is under 5; the closer to zero you are, the better.

Monthly debt_____ (include any new debt you are considering) / Monthly income_____ = _____

Leverage can also be calculated in equity and stocks, and it will tell you if you are ready to take on more debt. If your home is worth $100,000, but you only owe $50,000, then you have $50,000 in equity. Stocks are also calculated using this formula.

Gains and Losses (also known as "percentage of increase") = (Market Value - Purchase Price) / Purchase Price

Rate of Return = 72 / (Annual Rate of Investment)

Understanding these formulas will help you understand your money even better and, just like a successful romance, financial success involves communicating with your money.

<u>Week 26- Getting Rid of Financial Clutter</u>

This week, you will get rid of financial clutter. It is so easy to keep way more than you need and end up surrounded by receipts and statements that serve no purpose. The Clutter Commandments are as follows:

1. Only keep sales receipts until product warranties and/or return periods expire, or until you've filed taxes.
2. Only keep your ATM printouts until you reconcile your bank statements.
3. Only keep pay-stubs until you receive your W2s.
4. Only keep receipts for your utility bills until you receive the next bill--unless you have a home office, in which case you should keep those receipts for three years.
5. Only keep cancelled checks for one year, unless you need them for tax purposes.
6. Only keep credit card receipts for one year, unless you're using them for tax purposes.
7. Only keep bank statements for one year--three, if you need them for taxes.
8. Only keep your income tax statements for three years.
9. Keep marriage licenses and wills forever.
10. Keep records of selling a house for three years.
11. Keep stock records for as long as they are active.
12. Keep any contracts for as long as they are active.
13. Keep medical bills and cancelled insurance policies for three years.
14. Keep satisfied loans for seven years.

<u>Week 27- Investment Real Estate</u>

Real estate can be a great investment, if you're up for the challenge. The right real estate investment can be a great source of additional income and equity. This extra income is a great way to save for retirement and, once the home is paid in full, you have equity should you ever need it.

Real estate investments are like a project date; you have to help dress them, clean out their eyes, and help them find the right career, before you guys can live happily ever after. These relationships take work, but are worth it in the end. Just because your financial soul mate is not "All That" right now, does not mean that they are not capable of being all you ever dreamed of!

There are pros and cons to every investment. Real estate can be time consuming, especially if you try to handle all of the maintenance yourself--not to mention the taxes and tenants.

Investment real estate can be financed, but requires a higher down payment. In most cases, these down payments are anywhere between 20%-25% of the property's sale price and closing cost. Before you buy an investment property, it is very important that you ensure you have six months of payments stored away. You will need the cushion if you choose to finance the property for down periods when you are without a tenant, or when the property is in need of repairs. Trust me--at some point, the air conditioner will go out, a toilet will overflow, or you will need a plumber to repair a kitchen sink!

I would also suggest addressing the following when considering investment real estate:

1. Should I hire a management company to handle the repairs and rent collection, or can/should I do that myself?
2. Do I honestly have enough in savings to afford payments when I do not have a tenant?
3. Do I have 20% down, in addition to the closing cost to obtain the property?
4. Is my credit score above 640?
5. Could I be a cash buyer?
6. What is the property's projected rent? (hint: contact a realtor for this)
7. Have I contacted a real estate professional and a banker to determine if this would be the right type of investment for me?

Agencies such as the Housing Authority and the Veterans Housing Council are secrets to consider when investing in real estate--because, these agencies can act as liaisons who guarantee receipt of your monthly rent, as a landlord can receive payment directly from these agencies, instead of the tenants.

The average millionaire reportedly has seven sources of income. This week, your homework is to think about your multiple streams of income. This means that you will have income coming from different sources--not just a second job, but investments that help you save for your future.

Week 28- The Power of No!

Now that you are learning and understanding your money, you will soon find others noticing. Your family and friends can see a different confidence in you. It's called your Financial Glow! It's similar to the glow you get when you find a date you really like and you begin to smile more and carry yourself differently.

Just like in the dating world, "The Glow" can also attract people who want to know what you're doing and who you are doing it with. Your Financial Glow will attract people who are in need of financial help. People will want you to help pay bills, invest in businesses, or just loan them money for whatever reasons they can think. However, the truth is you don't have money to lend. If you still owe anyone money, you don't have money to lend. If you have a mortgage, car payment, credit card debit, or any other debt, you have obligations.

I understand: we are human, and it is hard for us to let family members and friends suffer so, in this regard, we are going to establish giving limits.

This week, you will set budgets for your loans--I mean "donations," because, let's be real; once your money leaves your hands, it's pretty much gone. This week, you will set limits so that these donations do not affect your overall financial health!

I, _____, will only loan or donate the following:

$_____ for fundraising. This includes all school, sports, fish plate fundraisers, etc. This does not include your tithes and offerings.

$_____ is what I can honestly afford to loan this year and still be able to pay my bills, save, and handle all of my other obligations.

$_____ birthday and Christmas and Anniversary. I know this one is a tough one, but do you realize how easy it is to over spend during these holidays? Most people find themselves buried in debt after the New Year, because they don't set a budget, which is not the way to start your year!

Week 29- Debt-to-Income Ratio and Credit Formulas

There is a formula for financial love, as there is for romantic love. A Debt-to-Income ratio, or DTI, is the percentage of a consumer's monthly gross income that goes toward paying debt. The formula for a happy relationship is: time + financial freedom + commitment + love. The formula for the Debt-to-Income ratio is your monthly debt payments divided by your gross monthly income.

Let's figure out your financial love formula:

A. **Monthly Debt Spend**
   Mortgage=
   Minimum credit card payments=
   Car loan=
   Student loans=
   Alimony/child support payments=
   Other loans/debt=
   Total= _____

B. **Total Monthly Income**
   Income from wages=
   Alimony/child support=
   Bonuses or overtime=
   Other income=
   Total=_____
   Debt-to-Income Ratio = (A÷B x 100 %)
   To calculate your Debt-to-Income ratio, divide your monthly debt (A) by your monthly income (B), then multiply by 100.

Your percentage will determine if you are financial dating material.

If you are 50% or more, consider yourself a bad date. You have a lot of work to do! Pay debts aggressively. You may even need to talk to someone quickly.

At 43%-49%, you are likely in financial hot water. You have too much baggage to really have a productive financial relationship. You need to pay off debts quickly to prevent getting overwhelmed and get rid of some of that baggage.

At 37%-42%, you are a good financial date, but you should really consider cleaning out your financial closet and paying down some debts, in order to make your financial relationship stronger.

At 36% or less, you are ready to mingle. You are a good financial date. Be sure to stay away from any additional debt. A moment on the card could be a lifetime on the credit report.

Week 30- Pay off Home early

Paying off your home early seems impossible, considering you signed up to pay it off in thirty years--but, it may be easier than you think! A home that's quickly paid for is a hard asset that leaves you with extra money for those emergency and play funds. This week is informational: just some things to think about.

Let's say you buy a home today for $200,000, with an interest rate 4.5%. If you made an initial payment and paid a twelfth of the subsequent payment, you would have paid your mortgage four years and four months early, which would save you around $27,000 in interest.

In the same scenario, you could also burn your mortgage at the same rate by simply making one extra payment a year. You could use your tax return to make these extra yearly payments or--if you are disciplined and paid biweekly--you could put the extra paychecks toward these payments

Never underestimate the power of a little bit extra because, just like when you're dating, a little extra goes a long way. Interest on your mortgage is compounded, which means that each month's interest is determined by the total amount owed (Monthly Interest = Principal Amount + Outstanding Interest.)

This week's goal is: Think About Action. Once you are financially free, how much extra will you commit to paying down your mortgage? I tell you: "Burn the Mortgage" parties are the best!

Complete the action that works best for you:

A. I will pay $1/12^{th}$ extra, each month, on my mortgage
B. I will make one extra payment, each month, toward my mortgage (13th payment)

C. I will pay a lump sum toward my mortgage. I will use funds from _____ to make this payment (hint: a tax return works as well.)

D. I will pay _____ extra on my mortgage each month-- this is for you go-getters who are ready to pay off your mortgage even faster.

Week 31- Home Equity Lines of Credit

Owning your home outright offers a sense of freedom. It's like when you reach the point in your dating journey when you become confident in who you are, and you refuse to settle for less. Burning the mortgage to your home can be one of the most profound moments in your life.

Last week, we established ways to pay off your mortgage early and bring you racing to that sense of freedom. Since there are some pros to keeping your mortgage, like being able to write off the interest on your taxes, I understand that some people might question why you would rush to pay it off. The realest answer to the question is, simply, equity. Remember, a home is a hard asset. A hard asset is something you can borrow against; it is collateral. It is called "hard" collateral because it can't be moved, and it usually maintains its value. Moving a house is arguably difficult.

Some benefits of paying your mortgage early are:

1. An equity line that is a great way to quickly source your emergency fund.
2. Monthly savings that you can put into an interest-bearing account, or retirement account.
3. Not having to stress about monthly payments.
4. A Home Equity Line that only requires payments on the amount of money you actually spend. For instance: if you have a $50,000 credit line, but you only use $1,000 of it, the $1000 is all you have to pay off.

To determine the amount for which you qualify in an equity line, you need to see how much equity you have in your home. The equity is the amount your home is worth minus the amount you owe. Now, realize, the price you paid for your home may not be the amount your home is currently worth. Good references for what your home may be worth are: your tax card, past sales of similar homes, and current prices of comparable homes in your area. Contact your financial institution to see the lending percentage for which you qualify. Some banks will allow you 85% to 90%. This means that if your home is worth $100,000 and you owe $50,000 then, at 85%, you can borrow up to $85,000. Subtract the $50,000 from the $85,000 to get the line amount of $35,000.

This week, your homework is to determine the worth of your home; the amount you owe; and, the amount of equity in your home. If you have a fair amount of equity, contact your local bank to determine if you qualify for an equity line. This equity line is not to spend but, rather, to have in case of an emergency.

I owe _____.

My home is worth_____.

This means I have _____ in equity.

Week 32- 529 Accounts and College Savings Accounts

A 529 Plan account is a financial mate that will love your kids as much as it loves you. These accounts are operated by a state or education institution to allow you to set aside funds for future college expenses. These accounts were created in 1996 and are named after Section 529 of the IRS Code.

Nearly every state has a 529 account to which you can contribute so you can take advantage of these accounts for your children, wherever you are. There are many benefits to enrolling in a 529 account.

1. The plan grows, is federal and tax-free, and will not be taxed when the money is taken out to pay for your child's college education.
2. Thirty-four states, including the District of Columbia, offer full or partial tax deductions to residents who contribute to the plan.
3. In most cases, the children have no legal rights to the money, which means you get to stay in control and ensure that funds are used for school and not the latest gear!

4. These accounts are low maintenance "set and let" accounts, for which contributions can easily be automatically drafted.

5. Since you do not have to report contributions on your federal tax return, you will not receive a 1099--and, we could all use fewer tax documents.

6. Funds can be rolled over, into another 529 plan, once a year, which is great if you have multiple children.

Certain plans have lifetime limits on contributions, which can range from $235,000 to $400,000.

Week 33- Meet the Family- Introducing Your Kids to Money and Allowances

This week is important if children are a future possibility for you; if you already have kids; or, if you are an aunt or an uncle who plays a significant role in a child's life.

It's time to introduce your kids to your money! I know, I know, you're not sure if it's true love yet. I mean, you guys really just started dating. You're not sure if you are exclusive or if you're in a long term relationship but, the reality is: your kids are ready to meet your money. They already have a feeling about your money; they know a lot more than they put on. Your kids have watched your old money habits, which is why you need to address what habits they understand, and what habits they might need to understand. You know the talk; it's the "do as I say, not as I have done" or the "be better than I was" talk. Remember, your kids are a reflection of you, in most cases--and, if they have seen you struggle, or handle your money in certain ways, they are likely to mimic your financial behaviors. Have a conversation with your kids about your money and what they can do better.

So, when you introduce your kids to your money, make them comfortable and make it fun. Teach them how to save for things they want now, and how to save for the future. The 529 Accounts from earlier are saving for college--the lessons from now are about spending money for now.

Here are some creative ways to teach your kids to save:

Allowances - Give your kids a weekly allowance, but have them budget portions for needs, wants, and rainy days. This teaches them how to manage their paycheck later in life. Money habits can last a lifetime.

Change Jar/Piggy Bank - I use this with my little ones. It can be a great lesson on how to count change, and you would be surprised at how excited it makes them to cash in the coins at the change collector. Once you cash in the coins, be sure to put a portion into a savings account, and get them something great with the rest.

Chores for Cash - There is nothing like a "work for it" attitude. Give your little moneymaker a list of chores to be completed to earn cash, then have them divide their well-earned funds into a budget for needs, wants, and savings. This will teach responsibility and great saving habits. Most kids appreciate their money more when they work hard for it.

Who knows--next thing you know, your kids will be falling in love all by themselves. They grow up so fast!

Homework: This week, introduce your money to your little spender. Design a way for them to start their own financial relationship. Remember, an allowance can be as small as a dollar or five dollars; don't overcommit and find yourself unable to fulfill the payment plan. Your kids might miss the whole point of budgeting if you don't adhere to a realistic plan of your own.

Week 34- Don't Suffocate Your Money

This week, we are going to work really hard to not be too clingy. We all know how it goes we start digging someone and, the next thing you know, we are calling and wanting to be with that person all the time. This can happen with your money. You can absolutely suffocate your money! You will find yourself constantly checking accounts, counting coins, and not giving your money a chance to grow. I totally understand that you're happy to see it there, and you want to keep it safe--but, in order for the relationship to grow, you have to trust your money, your broker, your financial advisor, and your bank. However, that doesn't mean you can't do your check registry, or check your account balances, etc. I am simply saying that when your money is in your brokerage account, don't get scared when your balance goes down or if you need to sell. Your broker has you covered. Now, if you feel that you want to be more or less aggressive, that is a conversation to be had, and watching the markets online is a great idea. However, if you panic and decide to remove your money from certain accounts, or consistently doubt your financial advisor, working together might be difficult for the two of you. Your obsessive financial behavior is no different from the date who constantly calls or texts you, needing to know every move you make. That behavior makes you back away because you feel like that person does not trust you. This is why it is very important to financially date your broker before putting all of your eggs in one basket. You should be a player. Sow your financial oats and contact several brokers before settling down with one.

Here are some quick tips to ensure you don't suffocate your financial wingman:

1. Ask questions that will make you feel comfortable with them managing your money.
2. Ensure that your advisor is licensed and bonded with the proper authorities.
3. Be sure you take the time to understand what you are investing in, and ask for a prospectus.
4. Ask if your broker is a fiduciary; fiduciaries put your interests before their own. They disclose all of their fees upfront and let you know how they are paid. They also let you know of any current or possible future conflicts. Non-fiduciaries may be paid to sell a certain product.

Week 35- Let's Go on a Trip Together

One day, you will look at your money and want to get away. You're falling in love, and who wouldn't want to go on a trip with their love bug? When vacationing with your money, there are a few tips you should know.

1. Plan your trip in advance, so you have time to save for it.
2. Always make sure you have cash available.
3. Make sure you have a credit card for backup.

We all need to get away from time to time and, there are ways to do this--but, we have to ensure we are meeting all of our other obligations. A vacation is always great project for your financial vision board. Place your next trip on your board and start saving for takeoff!

This week, pick a destination for you and your financial sugar pie. You will contact a travel agent for an estimate on the cost of the vacation. Once you have your destination, you will set up a financial vision board and start planning your trip.

1. Pick a destination. I want to travel to _____
2. Contact a travel agent: _____
3. Price your vacation. It will cost $_____
4. Spending money needed: $_____
5. Commit to saving $_____ per month until takeoff to accomplish my goal.

Week 36- How do I buy a house... and how much can I buy?

Some of us are looking for long term relationships when we date. A long term financial relationship is called a Mortgage. You guys can be stuck together for thirty years or fewer--maybe more, if you choose to refinance or cash out your equity. That's right, some people marry their mortgage. Homeownership is a goal for most of us. No matter if you want to purchase an additional home, or your first home, it is important to know how much "house" will not make you "house poor." Yes, I said, "house poor!" We have all fallen in love with the big, expensive house with all the upgrades and all of the new shiny appliances, and immediately started imagining all the sacrifices we were willing to make to be able to afford it--after all, do we *really* need food or clothes? But, the truth is that you should only ever purchase a home that makes financial sense.

A new home should be no more than 3 times your yearly salary. Remember, your home is a place for you to relax, not a place of stress. Most people's homes are foreclosed because they didn't completely understand their loan program, or because they bought a home that was wildly out of budget. Your emergency fund is a big part of your homeownership, and should hold 6 months of payments. Be sure you understand your payments and if you can afford the home in question.

The most important thing to be when applying for a mortgage is "prepared." The following are what you should have when applying for a mortgage:

1. 2 years of tax returns
2. Your current W2's
3. Current paystub

These things are important to help the mortgage officer determine how much "home" you can afford. Please highlight this: YOU MAY BE ABLE TO AFFORD SOMETHING ON PAPER, BUT ONLY **YOU** KNOW WHAT YOU CAN TRULY AFFORD! Paper doesn't always reveal your true spending habits. For instance, what's "on paper" might not reflect your children's activities, your shoe addiction, or your need to see the world. It's easy to say, "I just won't do these things," or "I might have to sacrifice to get the home I want," but unrealistic thinking will make you House Poor. Being House Poor means that you can **only** afford your home--but, you cannot afford to live your life. When buying a home, it is important to remain true to yourself.

1. 3 times my salary equals_____.
2. The amount of "house" I feel that I can afford monthly is _____.

Remember, there is more to owning a home than the mortgage. It is important to know that, as a homeowner, you will have taxes, maintenance, and insurance expenses. Your mortgage professional will be able to help you determine the best option moving forward.

Mortgage soul mates are just like dating soul mates; you have to pick the right one to have a happy ending. There are two main types of mortgages: conventional and Federal Housing Administration (FHA). A conventional mortgage is a mortgage offered and backed by a financial institution. It usually requires more money down and a higher credit score. An FHA mortgage is back by the government and only requires 3.5% down on purchase of your new home and a 620 credit score, as of 2016.

Week 37- Hey Baby, What's Your Name?

Have you ever seen a person so fine you think, "I've got to have them?" I mean, great body, great smile, great personality--the whole package. Well, some people feel this way about cars and, while it is okay to look at nice cars, you have to be sure you check the price tag and the engine before purchasing.

Cars are depreciable assets, and you should be very careful when purchasing one. A depreciable asset is something that loses its value rapidly. Once you drive off the lot, the value of the car drops.

Let's say, you purchase a car for $15,000; your credit status is excellent (meaning your score is 700 or above); your estimated interest rate is 5%; and, your payment is only $352 a month. If you have "good" credit, your payments could be $391 at an interest rate of 10%. However, if you have "fair" credit, your payments might be $427 at an interest rate of 15%. This is why it is important to make sure you have all of your credit affairs in place before purchasing your new car. Having your credit affairs out of whack could mean having to pay a lot of money, in the end.

This week, you will see if you can afford the car you have been eyeballing for a while now.

1. Determine how much of a monthly payment you are comfortable with paying.
2. Research the maintenance cost on the car you want. There is nothing worse than buying a car whose maintenance you can't afford.
3. Research the resale or trade-in value of the vehicle.
4. Determine the interest rate you qualify for and determine the total amount you will pay. Remember, never finance a car for over 3 years. Places will offer you up to 7 years, but you will be upside-down in your payments.
5. Pay cash, if you can. Not having to pay interest on your new car makes a huge difference in your financial world.

Week 38- Wills

This week, I have an important question for you: do you have a Will? I know, nobody wants to think about death, which is probably why 70% of Americans do not have a Will! If you have dependents, this is especially important--no matter how much, or how little, you own. You can create a Will with computer software like WillMaker, or websites like Legalzoom and Willing.com. You could also speak with an attorney if your situation is complicated and you feel you need further advice.

Remember, you have now saved to get your money in the right place, and you want your family or friends to enjoy it if you can't, so here are some things you should consider when making a Will:

1. Are 18 years of age or an emancipated minor? ————————————
2. Are you in your right mind, or of sound mind? _____
3. Do you know what a Will is and what it does?_____
4. Do you understand the relationship between you and your immediate family members?_____
5. Do you know all the property you own, and all of your assets? ————
6. Do you know who your beneficiaries are? _____
7. Be sure you recognize and state that this document is your Will!

   _____
8. Be sure you sign and date the Will!_____
9. You must have the Will signed (*attested*) by, at least, two or three witnesses – the number of required witnesses depends on state law. Also consider that many states require that the witnesses are not related to you and are not beneficiaries.
10. Nominate a legal guardian for any minor children, if needed_____
11. Make a list of who gets what, and who inherits specific items_____
12. You must tell what will happen to remaining assets not mentioned in the Will.
13. You must appoint an Executor of your Will. This person will be responsible for supervising the distribution of property and paying all of your debts and taxes. _____

The worst thing you can do is leave your family in uncertainty. This would cause a rift in your family and force court battles that could be avoided if you just set forth a plan to help your family understand your wishes after death.

Week 39- Everyone Loves Gifts- How to date your spouse and your money?

Every so often, we are required to buy gifts. These gifts can be large or small, expensive or inexpensive, depending on the taste of the recipients--some of the smallest boxes can carry some of the most expensive gifts!

If you are a person who likes to purchase gifts, it is important that you set a dating allowance each month and stick to it. Remember that holiday months require higher monthly allowance limits, so you may have to make sacrifices in other areas, such as eating out and clothing for that month. You could also try more personal dates, like staying in, cooking your date a nice meal, and renting a movie. You would be surprised at how far a picnic, or a Movie and Chill, would get you. I know this is not something you would do every time, but think of creative ways that you could save money.

This week, think about your budget and how much you could save by being creative during dating and gift-giving.

List 5 creative dates:

1. _____
2. _____
3. _____
4. _____
5. _____

Week 40- How to save for wants- Nothing wrong with wanting

We all have wants! Desire is what keeps the world going, honestly. We all *need* water--but, we might *want* a nice cold drink. You have to want. For some of us, desires are the motivation that keep us faithful to our financial relationships and our work. There is a proper way to save for your wants that will ensure you are able afford what you want, while maintaining your relationship with your financial soul mate:

1. Make a budget and stick to it. This allows you to save for, and prioritize, your wants.

2. Layaway is also a good option when looking to purchase something. This way, the item is secured and you can make payments, without interest, over a period of time.
3. Charge it on a card--no, you didn't misread; you can purchase the item on a low-interest credit card, as long as the item won't take the card's balance over 30%. Then, make an aggressive plan to repay the debt.

Trust me, we all want things--but, be sure the things you want fit into your budget. There is nothing worth ruining your credit for.

This week's homework is to name 5 things you want, and come up with specific plans to secure them.

1. _____
2. _____
3. _____
4. _____
5. _____

Week 41- Shoe, Clothes, and Toys Budget

This week, I want to focus on your spending. Your spending is one of the hardest things to tackle when learning to deal with your money. As I've said before, your money is a mindset, and you have to think of how important it is to you and your family.

When you date someone, they date your family. The two of you will not always be alone. There will be family functions. Your family will need you. Some may even need to crash with you, from time to time. This is why it is important that your soul mate and your financial soul mates are in harmony.

This budget will help you manage your spending and save portions of your budget for the things you want out of life, like shoes and other expensive items. Your Toy Budget is important in the relationship because we all want to have fun--it's human nature, and you can't take away the things that make you "you" during this process.

This week, your homework is to think of five things you want. Write down these five things and start putting the Toy portion of your budget to work. If you still have credit card debt, please take care of that first before you start purchasing your wants. We work hard and we all deserve rewards but, remember, being financially free is the best reward you can get.

Five things you want to buy with your creative budget:

1. _____
2. _____
3. _____
4. _____
5. _____

Week 42- Finances and Love Connections

At this point in your journey, you are starting to feel free. You have extra spending money; you have saved to feel comfortable as life comes at you; you have followed a budget; you and your money are now getting to know one another better; and, you have developed a "best friend" type of relationship.

It is important to realize that you don't have to stress over your money anymore. Being financially free is also great for your dating relationship, no matter if you are with a spouse or a significant other. Financial difficulty is one of the leading reasons for divorce. Couples argue over finances more than any other subject. This week, we are introducing your spouse to your new financial love connection, and showing them that it is great for your relationship to be financially freaky.

Your spouse may be good with their money, but you need to establish how the two of you can come together to ensure that the household runs smoothly.

1. Be honest with your spouse about how much money you have saved and how much you both need for an emergency fund.
2. Establish ways you can work together to form a savings team. Your spouse can be a great financial teammate by adding to your emergency fund. A couple that saves together stays together.

3. Open communication by talking about your financial goals. Your spouse may want to pay off the home early, just like you, and you can work together to meet this common goal.
4. Communicate any debts you have and how your spouse can be your accountability partner as you pay off this debt.
5. Your spouse can also motivate you to reach your financial goals.

This week, your homework is to write down 5 things you believe your spouse can help you with, financially. This things can be as simple as being a shoulder to cry on, or being an accountability partner.

1. _____
2. _____
3. _____
4. _____
5. _____

Week 43- Diversify Your Assets

This week, let's take a look at your 401(k) and reduce any company stock to 10%. In the dating world, we call this "not putting our eggs in one basket." I mean, you're not married to your job, are you?

Mutual funds and Exchange-Traded funds (ETFs) are great for retirement savings, because they own dozens of stocks in their portfolios. They are like financial speed dating; they offer many lower-risk options.

All the investment options in your 401(k) can be a little overwhelming. A great option to look for is a "target retirement" or "life cycle" fund. Make sure you pick the specific portfolio that aligns with your expected retirement age. If you're 30, now, and you plan to retire at 65, look for the retirement plan options that are 35 years out--such as a 2051 plan. Then, you will have invested in a mix of stock and bond funds that are on schedule and fit for your age. Remember that "target retirement" funds are also good for your Roth IRA. Consider these funds as a financial "swingers" club, with all of these different funds in one bed together. There is nothing wrong with discovering your financial freaky side!

This week, look at what funds you are investing in your 401(k).

1. Think about when you want to retire.
2. Look for a "target date" fund to reflect that date.
3. Lower your company stock to 10%.
4. Watch your money grow!

Week 44- Keys to a Long Term Relationship!

There are tricks to ensuring a smooth financial journey. Below are some to help you stay in love with your money.

1. Freeze your credit cards. Place your cards in a bowl of water and freeze them. When you're ready to buy something, you will have thaw out your cards. This gives you time to think about the purchase.
2. Stick to your budget! It is important to stick with your budget to watch your money grow and become more attractive.
3. Be open with your money. Be truthful and understand that your money will love you back.
4. Don't overspend. Make sure you don't go crazy with your new financial freedom.
5. Live under your financial means. Live like you don't have it.
6. Just say no, if you don't have extra to lend.
7. Create multiple streams of income.
8. Keep your change--pennies make dollars!

This week, you will make a plan and conscious efforts to stay on course. Remember, finance is a mindset. When you live under your budget, you will be prepared for all of the ups and downs that life will throw at you.

Week 45- Formulas to continue success: 25% Savings- 50% Needs- 25% Wants and Giving

The keys to a great financial future are more accessible than you might realize. Just like it is important that you keep dating your romantic mate to keep the relationship fresh, you have to give your money the same type of attention.

Remember, 25% of your money should go to savings. It doesn't matter if it goes to a 401K, IRA, Brokerage account, or a money market savings account; it will need to be placed in a divided gaining account.

50% of your money should go to bills and other needs. As you continue to pay off debt, you may discover that you don't need 50% of your income to service your debts. In that case, you can increase your savings--and, maybe get in a want or two from it. Remember, retirement may not be as far away as you'd think.

The remaining 25% of your money should go to your wants, and giving. 10% of your money should go to the giving pot, and 15% should go to the things you want. 15% may not be enough to cover what you want, so you might have to save for a period of time to get the things you want.

Homework for this week is simple: map out your forever budget and set your financial boundaries.

Each paycheck can be broken down as follows:

25%= $_____
50%=$_____
25%=$_____

Knowing what is available to you to spend will help you make the best financial decisions. Living financially free is a choice, and it's up to you to set a budget, pay down debt, and enjoy life. Nobody likes to hang with the broke friend or broke mate.

Week 46- Keeping the Spice in Your Financial Relationship

Keeping the spice in your financial relationship is important. There are ways to make your money interesting and, this week, we are going to discover ways to make extra money while having fun. This week, we are tapping into a side of our money that we may not visit a lot.

To keep your financial relationship spicy, you can try the following:

1. Penny Stocks - They are a low-risk introduction to the stock market. Have fun trading and choosing stocks. Who knows, you may pick a winner!
2. Network Marketing - Network Marketing is a cool way to earn money while doing something you already love. For instance, booking vacations

could be a great choice if you are a traveler. You could earn money booking trips for others, as well as telling them all about your experiences. In some cases, you could earn free trips! These opportunities usually have low start-up costs and can be great sources of income.

3. Start a Financial Savings Club- It's always cool to save with friends. These groups are set to help you help each other save for vacations and other big expenses. Sometimes, when groups reach their goal, they have some sort of celebration--and, who doesn't like a good party!

Week 47- Life will happen

We all know: life happens. Just when everything is going well, the tire goes flat; you get sick; your air conditioning needs to be serviced, etc. We have all experienced the hard times of life. When you and your money are in a relationship, your money will take care of you during these times. The most important thing to remember when life gives you lemons is that you must continue to save after you've moved past your setback. Remember, the emergency fund is there to help during these moments--but, life happens again and again, and you will need to be prepared then, as you are now.

This week is all about being prepared.

Week 48- Doing Something Different- Entrepreneurship

Some of us get the entrepreneurship itch! If you've dreamed of owning a business, there are a few things you can do to be sure your financial soul mate is happy while you become the entrepreneur you always dreamed.

1. Start out working on your business part-time so you can use your current income to build your income.
2. Make sure you have the following in place before you leave your current company:
    a. Life insurance
    b. Healthcare
    c. Accidental insurance

3. 1 year of finances put away. If you are starting your business and you have a significant drop in income, you want to be financially able to ride the wave.

4. Have a business plan. I know people say you should leap and find your wings, but it's a better idea to jump with a parachute.

5. Secure a business mentor to help you along the way.

6. Contact a local banker to set up your business accounts. Ask about their loan products, and checking and savings options.

7. Obtain good software, like Quickbooks, that will assist you in keeping your financial documents together.

8. Know your business and check for ways to cut costs--for example, if you are a t-shirt designer, ensure you are getting a great wholesale deal on the actual shirts and that the quality is up to your standards.

9. Hire an accountant to help you during tax season. You might have several write-offs and deductions a trained professional could help you identify.

10. Maintain the integrity of your business. Never overbook.

Week 49- Great Resources- You can't talk about your relationship with everyone

Finding your financial soul mate can be quite difficult. You have done a great job at this financial dating game but, just like you can't tell everyone about your personal relationships, you also can't tell everyone about your finances. When you discuss your finances with someone other than a financial advisor, bad things can happen. Now, you might feel this doesn't apply to you, because you may have gotten good advice from a loved one before--but, when things go wrong, bad advice can ruin relationships.

When you vent to your friends after a fight with your partner, your friend gets angry on your behalf, and they might not forgive your partner as easily as you do when you decide you want to reconcile with your partner. Your friend might even reference that incident the next time you and your partner have a disagreement. This happens in the financial world, too: you tell someone about your money, and they formulate an opinion from there. The best thing for you to do is get you a financial best friend or wingman (aka an accountant), and a broker (aka a financial GodFather.)

Week 50- Financial Advisors - Your Financial Best Friend

Even though we now have a Love Jones for our money, it's important that we have an accountability partner to let us know if, financially, we are continuing in the right direction.

Your Financial Advisor is the best friend and accountability partner. You tell him or her all about your money, and he or she will tell you if you're in the right financial relationships. Make sure you choose this best friend carefully. You want to look at their history and ensure they have a good track record. We have all been burned by a friend before and, unfortunately, this can happen in the financial world as well. Take the time to research financial advisors in your area before taking their advice. It is important that this financial relationship is a trustworthy one.

Time to get down! Choose 5 potential financial best friends in your area. Set up a meeting with each one to evaluate how they can help you stay in love with your finances. These services come at a cost so, be sure you ask their fees and/or how are they paid. This will determine who you use.

	Firm	Number	Date Night
1.			
2.			
3.			
4.			
5.			

Week 51- Accountants- Your Wingmen in Financial Dating

Have you ever wondered if you need an accountant to manage your finances? Some people wear that they use the services from an accountant as a badge of honor. Well, if you are a business owner, or have investment properties or any other complex tax needs that will require a bookkeeper and tax advice, you may need an accountant. Accountants can service multiple purposes, but their main function is to create and review financial documents. Just like in the dating world, we all need a wingman to help us out of holes we may have dug ourselves into. Your accountant is your wingman. They will help you with your taxes and advise you on any important financial information. Often, people buy bookkeeping software, such as Quickbooks, to keep financial records. Your accountant will review these records and prepare your tax documents based on them.

Get ready for action. If you need an accountant, please write down 5 potential financial wingmen.

	Name of Firm	Phone
1.		
2.		
3.		
4.		
5.		

Week 52- YOU AND YOUR MONEY ARE NOW IN LOVE!!!

Dearly Beloved, YOU DID IT! You and your money are now whole. You guys can live in holy financial matrimony! You now understand your money, and you can live in financial bliss. Just like any other relationship, a financial relationship will remain intact if you listen to your money, communicate, seek advice from someone who truly knows the answers, and remain faithful to your financial circumstances. What does remaining faithful mean? Don't go out and overspend because you now have a better credit score and more money in the bank! Stay true to the principles, and you will do great! I am so happy for you and your money! May you and your financial soul mate live happily ever after!

Action--I know you didn't think you were off the hook? Write down 5 financial principles you learned from the last 52 weeks that you will continue to work on in the future. This will help you reference your struggle areas and help you when you're feeling weak--because, like every relationship, you and your money will have your ups and downs.

51

	Lesson	Page
1.	_____	_____
2.	_____	_____
3.	_____	_____
4.	_____	_____
5.	_____	_____
6.	_____	_____